101 AMAZING *Kitten & Cat* FACTS

BELLANOVA

MELBOURNE · SOFIA · BERLIN

Copyright © 2026 by Jenny Kellett
Cover image Photo by Tobi from Pexels
www.bellanovabooks.com

All rights reserved. No part of this book may be reproduced in any form by any electronic or mechanical means including photocopying, recording, or
information storage and retrieval without permission in writing from the author.

Imprint: Bellanova Books
ISBN: 978-619-264-067-5

CONTENTS

Foreward 4
Introduction 6
Cat Facts 8
Cat Quiz 70
Quiz Answers 75
Word search 76
Solution 78
Sources 79

FOREWARD

Thank you for buying my latest book. As a lifelong cat lover, I had so much fun researching and writing this book, and I hope you enjoy reading it!

Of course, I have to thank my wonderful cats for their daily laughs and inspiration.

— Jenny

My cats Lulu und Panda.

INTRODUCTION

It's hard not to love cats. In fact, more than one in every four families in the USA has at least one cat!

But how much do you really know about your cat?

In this book, you will learn over 100 amazing facts about the fabulous feline. From the hairless Sphynx cat to internet celebrity Grumpy Cat, you'll be a cat expert in no time!

Are you ready? Here we go!

A Russian blue.

KITTEN & CATS *Facts*

Like a human fingerprint, a cat's nose has a unique ridged pattern that can be used to identify them.

• • •

When cats are in a bad mood, they thrash their tails back and forth—so it's a good idea to leave them alone! Dogs do this when they're happy.

• • •

Cats spend around 30 percent of their time awake cleaning themselves.

A Siamese kitten.

Cats can make over 100 different sounds, whereas dogs can only make 10.

• • •

Cats often squeeze their eyes shut when they are happy.

• • •

Ever wondered why companies don't sell mouse-flavored cat food? When scientists tested it, cats didn't like it!

A cat's average body temperature is warmer than a human's at around 101.5 °F (38.6 °C).

A Birman kitten.

Adult cats have 32 teeth; 16 on the top, 14 on the bottom.

• • •

Cats are very lazy—they sleep around 16 hours a day!

• • •

Do you know how old your cat really is? If she is 3, then in human years, she is 29! If she is 8, then she is 49 in human years.

• • •

It has been proven that having a purring cat sitting on your lap can help to relieve stress.

Amazing Kitten and Cat Facts

Cats have the largest eyes of all mammals relative to their size.

• • •

Cats like to eat grass because it helps them digest their food and remove fur in their stomachs.

• • •

Around 37 percent of Americans own at least one cat.

• • •

Domestic cats can run up to 30 miles per hour (48 km/h)!

Cats with blue eyes and white fur are often deaf.

• • •

Cats use their tails to balance themselves.

• • •

Cats have very sensitive hearing—more sensitive than humans and dogs.

British longhair.

Amazing Kitten and Cat Facts

Female cats are usually pregnant for around nine weeks, compared to humans, who are pregnant for nine months!

• • •

The official name for cat lovers is an **ailurophile**! Are you an ailurophile?

• • •

Cats not only purr when they are happy, they may also purr when they are in pain.

• • •

When your cat rubs up against you, it means she is claiming ownership of you—so take it as a compliment!

A black and white domestic shorthair. They are often called "tuxedo" cats!

A 3-month-old British Shorthair kitten.

Cats are lactose intolerant. This means that you shouldn't give them cow's milk, cheese, or chocolate as it can make them very sick.

• • •

Ancient Egyptians believed that the goddess Bast was the mover of all cats on Earth. They also believed that cats were sacred.

• • •

During its life, a female cat could have more than 100 kittens. It's important to spay and neuter your cats to stop unwanted pregnancies.

A ginger tabby doing what cats do best—cleaning!

Amazing Kitten and Cat Facts

A Scottish Fold cat. Notice the folded-over ears!

Sir Isaac Newton, who discovered gravity, also invented the cat flap!

• • •

The most popular cat names in the USA are Missy, Misty, Muffin, Patches, Fluffy, Tabitha, Tigger, Pumpkin, and Samantha. Is yours on the list?

• • •

If your cat likes to climb your Christmas tree, try hanging a lemon or orange-scented air freshener in the branches, as cats don't like this smell.

Amazing Kitten and Cat Facts

Cats are slightly color-blind; they can't tell the difference between green and red.

• • •

Cat's vision isn't that good at seeing detail—you probably appear blurry to them.

• • •

The color of a kitten's eyes changes as it gets older.

• • •

When kittens are born, they can't see or hear. Their eyes open at five days old, and their hearing and sight develop when they are around two weeks old.

A Scottish fold with a long coat is known as a Highland fold.

Amazing Kitten and Cat Facts

A group of adult cats is called a **clowder**.

• • •

Cats can't be vegetarians—they need protein from meat to survive.

• • •

Never feed your cat dog food; cats require five times more protein than dogs to stay healthy.

• • •

The average cat weighs 12 lbs (5.4 kg). How much does yours weigh?

This British Shorthair shows us her long tongue.

AMAZING KITTEN AND CAT FACTS

A calico-colored cat.

Cats are considered to be overweight if you can't feel their ribs.

• • •

The smallest cat ever recorded was Tinker Toy from Illinois. He weighed 1 lb 8 oz (0.6 kg) and was just 2.75 inches (7 cm) tall!

• • •

A cat's normal pulse is 140–240 beats per minute, with an average of 195. This is nearly twice as fast as a human.

• • •

Domestic cats are the only species that are able to hold their tails straight upward while walking.

Cats can jump seven times their own height.

• • •

While many parts of Europe and North America consider the black cat to be a sign of bad luck, in Britain and Australia, black cats are considered lucky.

• • •

Every year, approximately 40,000 people are bitten by cats in the USA.

• • •

It is important to spend lots of time playing with your kitten when he or she is very young so that they don't develop a fear of people.

A cat feeding her kittens.

An American curl.

Female cats can begin mating when they are between five and nine months old.

• • •

All domestic cats have the same ancestor—the African wild cat—which still exists today.

• • •

Cats can be both right-pawed and left-pawed, just like humans.

• • •

Cats are the only animals that have retractable claws.

Amazing Kitten and Cat Facts

If your cat snores or rolls over and shows you her belly, it means she trusts you.

• • •

The Ancient Egyptian word for cat was 'mau', which means 'to see'.

• • •

Kittens, like humans, are born with baby teeth, which are replaced by permanent teeth when they are around six months old.

Cats have a unique way of communicating through scent marking. They do this by rubbing their cheeks, chin, or head against objects, leaving behind their scent. This helps to establish their territory and communicate with other cats. In addition, cats have scent glands in their paws, which they use to leave their mark when scratching. This behavior helps cats to communicate with other cats, signal their presence, and mark their territory.

• • •

Cats cannot see directly under their noses.

< A Ragdoll kitten.

An Abyssinian kitten. They are very loyal, but also very demanding!

Cats take between 20–40 breaths a minute.

• • •

There are around 100 different breeds of cats.

• • •

Scottish fold cats have cute fold-over ears!

• • •

Cats can live for more than 20 years, but on average, they live for 14 years.

• • •

Just like humans, cats can get asthma. Dust, smoke, and other air pollution can irritate your cat.

Amazing Kitten and Cat Facts

Cats with long, lean bodies are more likely to be outgoing, whereas stocky cats are more protective and vocal.

• • •

A cat's brain is more similar to a human brain than a dog's brain.

• • •

Cats rarely meow at other cats; they only meow at humans. They spit, purr, and hiss at other cats.

• • •

The Pilgrims were the first to introduce cats to North America.

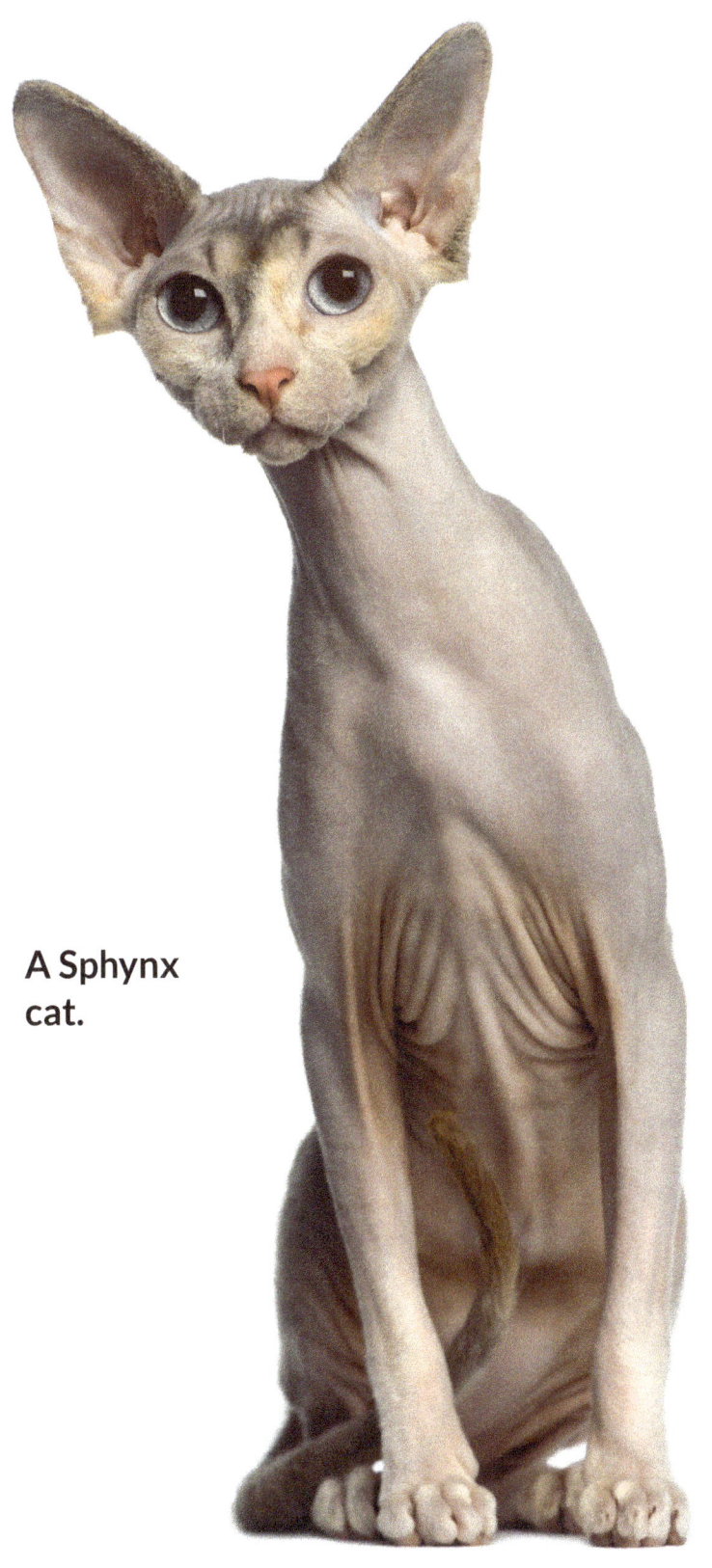

A Sphynx cat.

Amazing Kitten and Cat Facts

A cat called Dusty is recorded as having the most number of kittens; she had 420 in her lifetime.

• • •

In 1987, cats overtook dogs as the most popular pet in America.

• • •

Almost 10 percent of a cat's bones are in its tail.

• • •

The world's first cat show was in London in 1871. The first one in America was in 1895.

An American bobtail. Its very short tail is due to a genetic mutation. The first bobtail was discovered in Arizona in the 1960s.

A Bengal cat. They were originally a hybrid with an Asian Leopard cat, which gives them their wild appearance.

Cats step with both left legs, then both right legs when they walk or run.

• • •

The world's richest cat was Blackie, who was left $20 million by his owner, who passed away.

• • •

Cats walk on their toes.

• • •

Cats have a remarkable ability to always drink water cleanly and efficiently. Unlike dogs and other animals that tend to slobber and spill water all over the place, cats have a tongue that is specially adapted for drinking.

The surface of a cat's tongue is covered in tiny barbs that help to draw water into its mouth and prevent spills. This makes it possible for cats to stay clean and hydrated without making a mess.

• • •

Cats can't taste sweet things.

• • •

Most cats have no eyelashes.

• • •

Be careful what plants your cat gets to, as many are poisonous to them! English ivy, iris, mistletoe, and yew are all poisonous to cats.

Cats bury their poo to hide their scent from predators.

• • •

Kittens are taught to use a litter tray by their mothers, so it's important they stay with their mothers until they are at least nine weeks old.

• • •

Unlike humans, cats do not need to blink regularly to keep their eyes lubricated.

A Maine Coon kitten.

Amazing Kitten and Cat Facts

Some of the scariest men in history were afraid of cats! Julius Caesar, Charles XI, and Henry II all had a phobia of cats.

• • •

Even when cats sleep, they can tell when they are being touched. Try touching your cat's tail as she is sleeping, and you'll see her twitch!

Cats are likelier to respond to a name that ends in the sound 'ee'.

• • •

Abraham Lincoln loved cats. He had four of them living with him at the White House.

• • •

If you see two cats that live together rubbing heads, it means they're telling each other that they have no intention of fighting.

A Persian cat.

Cats have flexible spines and can rotate their ears 180 degrees. This gives them an incredible range of motion and allows them to hear sounds from all directions. The muscles in a cat's ear are also very strong and allow them to quickly and accurately pinpoint the source of a sound, making it easier for them to hunt or react to potential threats. This combination of a flexible spine and powerful ear muscles makes cats incredibly agile and aware of their surroundings.

• • •

Up to 60 million feral cats live in the United States alone.

A Maine Coon— one of the largest breeds of domestic cats.

Cats can get cancer. White cats should avoid going outside in the sunshine as they are more likely to get skin cancer.

• • •

Cats cannot produce fat, so they must have it in their diet.

• • •

Cats have around 130,000 hairs per square inch!

• • •

It is believed that cats don't think that they are little people. Instead, they see humans as big cats!

Cats have a third eyelid, called the "haw" or nictitating membrane, that protects their eye and keeps it moist. It closes diagonally across the eye and provides extra protection against dirt. A partially visible third eyelid can indicate a cat's health and well-being.

• • •

Cats can be taught to walk on a leash, but it takes time and is easiest if you start them off when they are very young.

• • •

On average, cats have 24 whiskers in four horizontal rows on each side of their faces.

Cats are very elegant and they're happy to show that off!

Having your cat neutered can increase its lifespan by up to three years.

• • •

Cats are able to predict when earthquakes will happen. Scientists aren't sure why, but they are currently studying it.

A Cornish rex.

Cats can't move their jaws sideways, which is why they can't eat large chunks of food. Always make sure your cat's food is well chopped up.

• • •

Cats can drink around five teaspoons of water every minute.

• • •

It is estimated that around 54 percent of cats in the USA are overweight. Make sure you feed your cat a healthy diet, rich in protein and low in fat. A typical cat only needs around 180–200 calories each day.

< **A ragdoll cat**

Amazing Kitten and Cat Facts

Your cat's front paws have five toes, whereas the back paws only have four. However, some cats, known as **polydactyl cats**, have more than the usual number of toes on one or more paws. This genetic variation is relatively common and is considered harmless.

• • •

Cats can hear mice's ultrasonic sounds, which helps them when hunting.

• • •

A cat's collar bone is not connected to any other bones; it is surrounded by muscle. This makes it easy for them to squeeze through tight spots.

A Norwegian forest cat.

Amazing Kitten and Cat Facts

Cats only have 473 taste buds; humans have over 9,000!

• • •

Cats can tell when you are angry at them by the tone of your voice.

Cats purr 26 times per second, which is why you hear the buzzing sound.

• • •

When cats are really happy, they knead with their paws.

• • •

In Macy's Thanksgiving Day parade, a Felix the Cat balloon was the first balloon ever used.

A Bengal.

Cats have a unique collarbone that allows them to always land on their feet. Unlike humans with a solid collarbone, a cat's collarbone is flexible and can move in a way that helps absorb the shock of a fall. This is why, even if a cat falls from a high place, it can twist its body midair and adjust its landing position so that it lands on its feet.

• • •

Cats have a special muscle in their eye that allows them to focus on objects and keep their eyes fixed on a target even while they are moving. This muscle is called the "lateral rectus muscle," and enables cats to have excellent visual hunting skills.

A British longhair.

Cats are believed to have been domesticated over 10,000 years ago in the Near East. They were kept as pets to control rodents and other pests in human settlements.

• • •

Unlike adult cats, which are usually solitary animals, kittens are very social and love to play and interact with their littermates. They use play to develop important skills, such as hunting and stalking.

The word "kitten" comes from the Middle English word "kitoun," which means "little cat."

• • •

Kittens have a very good sense of smell, which they use to identify their mother and littermates, as well as to locate food and potential dangers. Their sense of smell is so powerful that they can detect scents that are undetectable to humans.

A pregnant Sphynx   >

CAT *Quiz*

Now it's time to test your new feline knowledge! Answers are on page 75.

1 How many teeth does an adult cat have?

2 What do cats do when they are really happy?

3 Cats eyes change color as they get older. True or false?

4 What percentage of a cat's bones are in its tail?

5 How many breeds of cats are there?

6   Are cats left-pawed or right-pawed?

7   What is a group of adult cats called?

8   What is the scientific name for a cat lover?

9   How fast can cats run?

10   How many hours a day do cats sleep?

11   What does it mean when a cat thrashes its tail back and forth?

12   Who invented the cat flap?

13   What is the common ancestor of all domestic cats?

14 When are kittens baby teeth replaced by permanent teeth?

15 Cats can't see under their noses. True or false?

16 How long do cats live for, on average?

17 Who first introduced cats to North America?

18 Cats walk on the balls of their feet. True or false?

19 Why do cats bury their poo?

20 How many hairs do cats have per square inch?

ANSWERS

1. 32.

2. They knead with their paws.

3. True.

4. 10%.

5. Around 100.

6. They can be either!

7. A clowder.

8. An ailurophile.

9. Up to 30 miles per hour (48 km/h).

10. Around 16 hours a day.

11. It's in a bad mood.

12. Sir Isaac Newton.

13. The African wild cat.

14. When they are around seven months old.

15. True.

16. 14 years.

17. The Pilgrims.

18. False. They walk on their toes.

19. To hide their scent from predators.

20. 130,000.

Cats
WORD SEARCH

```
D S A K I O P A S F X A
V F D C S E J Q S E P I
P F R R A G D O L L F L
U Q L J A T X D N I D U
R J K I U A S S N N J R
R Z C L O W D E R E K O
I Q Y R W E W S A C W P
N Q K J S A W D F V A H
G J S L I W Q Z M Z Q I
D S P H Y N X R E E S L
R F E S A Q F N L W O E
Z X K I T T E N S X Z W
```

Can you find all the words below in the word search puzzle on the left?

CATS	RAGDOLL	CLOWDER
SPHYNX	PURRING	AILUROPHILE
MEOW	FELINE	KITTENS

Amazing Kitten and Cat Facts

SOLUTION

								F	A
			C					E	I
P			R	A	G	D	O	L	L
U				T				I	U
R					S			N	R
R		C	L	O	W	D	E	R	O
I									P
N									H
G							M		I
		S	P	H	Y	N	X		E		L
								O	E
		K	I	T	T	E	N	S		W

SOURCES

"Cat - Wikipedia". 2023. En.Wikipedia.Org. https://en.wikipedia.org/wiki/Cat.

"Cat | Breeds & Facts". 2023. Encyclopedia Britannica. https://www.britannica.com/animal/cat.

"50 Cat Facts You Probably Didn't Know". 2019. Georgia Veterinary Associates. https://www.mygavet.com/services/blog/50-cat-facts-you-probably-didnt-know.

"14 Mind-Blowing Facts About Cats | Purina". 2023. Purina.Co.Uk. https://www.purina.co.uk/articles/cats/behaviour/common-questions/fun-facts-about-cats.

"31 Fascinating Cat Facts To Make You The Master Of Feline Trivia ". 2023. Daily Paws. https://www.dailypaws.com/living-with-pets/pet-owner-relationship/facts-about-cats.

"Maine Coon - Wikipedia, La Enciclopedia Libre". 2023. Es.Wikipedia.Org. https://es.wikipedia.org/wiki/Maine_Coon.

"Guide To Cat Breeds". 2023. The Spruce Pets. https://www.thesprucepets.com/cat-breeds-4162123.

"10 Affectionate Cat Breeds You'll Fall In Love With". 2023. The Spruce Pets. https://www.thesprucepets.com/affectionate-cat-breeds-4846595.

"Sphynx Cat | Breed Of Cat". 2023. Encyclopedia Britannica. https://www.britannica.com/animal/Sphynx-cat.

"Abyssinian | Breed Of Cat". 2023. Encyclopedia Britannica. https://www.britannica.com/animal/Abyssinian.

"Scottish Fold Cat | Breed Of Cat". 2023. Encyclopedia Britannica. https://www.britannica.com/animal/Scottish-fold-cat.

We hope you learned some awesome facts about kittens and cats! Which was your favorite?

We'd love to hear from you in a **review**! Not only do they make us smile, but they help other readers choose their next book.

Looking for more amazing animal facts? Join us at
www.bellanovabooks.com
for the latest book releases and much more.

ALSO BY JENNY KELLETT

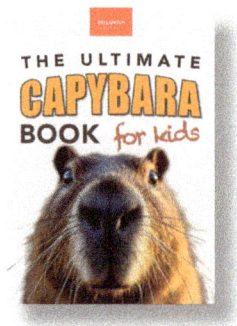  

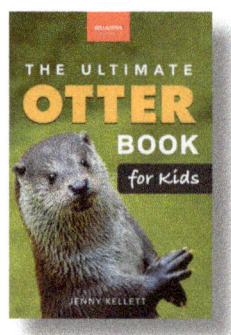  

... and more!

Available at
www.bellanovabooks.com
and all major online bookstores.

www.ingramcontent.com/pod-product-compliance
Lightning Source LLC
LaVergne TN
LVHW050842080526
838202LV00009B/314